Hafsa Abdur-Rahman is a poet and has previously had her first poetry book named Hafsa's Poems published, which was realised on 3rd March 2023. This would be her second poetry book.

Hafsa started writing from her teenage years and has always been fascinated with poetry. She finds writing therapeutic as well as relaxing.

I want to thank my mum and my dad, along with all my family and friends.

Hafsa Abdur-Rahman

POETRY FROM THE HEART

AUSTIN MACAULEY PUBLISHERS™
LONDON • CAMBRIDGE • NEW YORK • SHARJAH

Copyright © Hafsa Abdur-Rahman 2024

The right of Hafsa Abdur-Rahman to be identified as author of this work has been asserted by the author in accordance with sections 77 and 78 of the Copyright, Designs and Patents Act 1988.

All rights reserved. No part of this publication may be reproduced, stored in a retrieval system, or transmitted in any form or by any means, electronic, mechanical, photocopying, recording, or otherwise, without the prior permission of the publishers.

Any person who commits any unauthorised act in relation to this publication may be liable to criminal prosecution and civil claims for damages.

A CIP catalogue record for this title is available from the British Library.

ISBN 9781035833924 (Paperback)
ISBN 9781035833931 (ePub e-book)

www.austinmacauley.com

First Published 2024
Austin Macauley Publishers Ltd®
1 Canada Square
Canary Wharf
London
E14 5AA

I would like to thank Austin Macauley
for publishing my book.

1
A New Opportunity

Tears of sorrow
Tears of joy

When one becomes bewildered, startled and overjoyed
Great things are to happen

A selection of emotions all compiled into one
Memories flash back and forth

A selection of thoughts which seem real, although an illusion
Wonderful memories are to be made however forgotten

Positivity elevates and innovates selected memories

Wisdom is taught through life and learnt experiences
which strengthens and motivates our wellbeing as well as
enhance change for new changes to occur

Believe in yourself!

Great
Things
Will
Happen.

2
Contentment in the Heart

A lady felt melancholic, dismayed and dismal
Her voice never heard

One's contentment can only be established through one's own engagement and strong will
Aid is needed, of course

Positive attributes to think more joyous and not fret about things that will never be changed.

Life can be delightful and content and what we make of it
Never give up
Like the saying goes:
"When one door closes, another opens."

3
Happiness Within

Life is like a story
Sometimes we get our happy endings
However, sometimes we don't

We can however change our perception of life and make it better

Sometimes in life, we desire a certain aspiration/dream

Life can take you to unexpected places
It can bring you
Laughter,
Happiness,
Sadness,
Tears

Happiness comes from the heart
No one can make you happy but yourself

Having a companion or having family and friends can elevate your happiness
However, happiness comes from within.

4
A Loving Person

I can remember your dazzling smile
Even through tough and testing times
You kept it together

You were such a strong, courageous and loving person
Even though you have passed, you remain in our hearts

From my youth, I can remember your generosity and kindness
Which will never leave our hearts.

5
Living in the Past

Blame and feeling ashamed and belittled

You begin to feel enraged and sob

"You can't do this."
"You can't do that."

You feel trapped
Only one believes
what one hears

Feeling pessimistic
Life should not be that way

Good times are encountered through one's misery
One's thought of feeling exasperated and agitated

One questions, "Why do I feel this way?"

A matrimony from one's wrong decision
Fate will bring the right person
Patience is a key virtue, as without, it we are nothing.

6
The Girl that Wept

A girl was unsatisfied with herself
Cruel remarks scrutinised day by day

She had no self-worth
She wept and wept, and tears almost filled as if they were drowning down her cheeks

She started to think brighter, as life is what you make of it

She left her negative thoughts
Instead, she filled herself with elevated and merry thoughts

This had helped her rejoice at the fulfilment of her new happiness.

7
The Weeping Willow

A tree wept from season to season
The tree had a missing piece

Therefore, found no peace and a lack of contentment and reassurance

The tree would weep day and night
Until
One day, the weeping willow found a river where the tree's complexion of misery and disappointment diminished and weeping willow changed her complication to a blissful state

The weeping willow pondered and within time started to change her thoughts and within time changed, and her mood and thoughts were elevated to a positive perception and began to look at her bright future.

It doesn't matter what one has been through
One should remember happiness isn't also around the corner
However, sad days will not last
What we do defines us and one's freedom

8
Freedom at Last

Long days through hardship
Days, months and years

No realisation of oneself
Identity is key

Knowing who you are and no one to change you
Years taken for realisation

Freedom is calling out
Finally, liberty

Everybody scrutinising
One's identity

Ones perception of one's view should be non-judgemental

In some events, life can be cruel
However, there are blissful moments which you should remember

It doesn't matter what one has been through

One should remember happiness isn't also around the corner
However, sad days will not last

What we do defines us and one's freedom

9
Mili: My Companion

Mili is my best companion
She is full of excitement and energy

She brought peace to my melancholic days and enlightened my heart
She is an affectionate, caring and joyous cat

She is my companion for life
She hasn't just brought happiness to me but to others

Mili, you are my companion for life.

10
The War

Hundreds hidden and some civilians wanting to fight
The Great War was about to begin

Hiding from the soldiers
Civilians didn't want to get caught out

Mothers and children in their homes

Brave men decided to fight for their country
Patriotic for the love of their country

Tortured and beaten and mistreated all for the love and bravery for their country

Many deaths however
Many ruinous

Wives weeping for longing to see their loved ones
Some returned to see their loved ones
While others didn't get a chance to go back to their loved ones

Bravery took over and the soldiers decided to fight for their country.

11
Alone

Once married in a bitter relationship
Tears of sorrow and excitement of one's companion and partner

Emptiness remains
Putting on a brave face

A whisper of one saying, "Smile"
Bewildered of the day to come

Yuling from different direction belting out
children frolicking in their dazzling pink dresses

The elderly women bored out of their misery
Young women dancing scrutinising one another and trying to compete with one another

The groom appears late
Two rings exchanged
However, broken after one year.

12
A Sunny but Cloudy Day

The sun came out however hurt and all the other emotions out ruled the sun
You wept almost 10 years of disbelief and ignorance

You are still finding your steps
Days feel like months over days going quickly
Aware but not aware
The sun emphasises brightness, elevated emotions and allows those who haven't seen the sun to feel dismay
Although those who admire the winter still smile
However
It brings misery to others

Seasons affect our mood but from time to time
We should uplift our emotions regardless of what month, season, day or time

Although easier said than done

We should thrive with happiness, even if we don't feel it within, as you can make somebody's day with just a simple smile.

13
Autumn

Autumn leaves fluttering all around
It's as cold as the North Pole

Ice cream van playing the tune and circulating the estate
Nobody however wanting any ice cream

The clouds are sad and almost crying
Some days are happy
Some days are sad

The rain belting down as if there were no tomorrow
Another day is to come, and spring is near

Ready for flowers to bloom.

14
Friendship

Friendship is key
You may lose a friend, however gain another

You may not expect to lose those who you thought would be your friend for life
New friends can be gained
Who wouldn't you expect to accompany your friendship?
Would become your friend? It's not the quantity; it's the quality

One great friendship can overpower hundreds of disloyal friends.

15
Day by Day

Days of melancholy, morning and night
Free me from the emotions

My head felt as if clouds filled with the pressure of the rain about to get released, however still compressed and heavy and too much tension

Some days are better than some

Every emotion
Attached
Guilt
Happiness
Sadness
Amongst others

The unknown creates one's anxieties, phobias and so on
Happiness comes and goes on

Beautiful memories that are remembered from one's youth to adulthood

Visiting different countries amongst outings not overseas
Within adulthood, life can be stressful. You can be happy, sad and complicated

Happy memories are created

A different type of liberty is created

You can let your wings fly in every direction
Whether north, east, south or west.

16
The Void Within

Void is found through emptiness
Feeling something, however feeling empty

Anguish is created through your sorrow and from one's deceit

Only you can change the void within
Some happiness is within; however, bitterness remains

Satisfied but unsatisfied
Emotions ruminating all around and manoeuvres with how you feel

One day is better than the rest
Acceptance is needed from yourself and no other.

17
Lost

Lost between a range of opinions of others

Disappointment and disapproval of others
"Why do you do this that way?"

A girl disheartened from the bad decision that she makes, as this is not approved by others

She decides to follow her own path and see where life leads her, and that decision should be made by herself,
she should take pride in herself.

18
Surreal Feelings

Walking through the blissful sun, however misery in one's thoughts
Antagonised, agitated and feeling the emotion of anguish

Children frolicking in the park
grandparents pushing the prams past

The Park quite empty, although it felt as if there were a loud crowd
Feelings of distress wanting to feel the summer day, however feeling melancholic

Gathered by others, however feeling alone
The days of summer shorter. However, I feel as if I want the day to end

Surreal feelings and unexpected turns…

19
The Ongoing War

Children frolicking about, unaware of what is to happen
Grenades overpowering and ruining lives of families

Separation of partners and even grandparents away from their grandchildren
No uplifting spirit as calamity strikes after calamity

Some optimism as some flee their country to be able to survive
Heartbreak however as many are left behind and many divisions

"Why does this have to happen?"
Not aware of what is to happen from day to day

A song of their nation sang to give them spirit over the gloomy and dismayed days
Fear of never seeing a loved one and leaving their loved ones behind, not knowing whether they will ever be reunited.

20
Sharing the Night with a Beautiful Companion

It had gone past dusk; everything silenced
Only a tick of the clock

The blinds are halfway open with a beautiful, picturesque view
Trains passing through different times at night passing through
Which I spot out my window around dusk onwards

I share the night with a beautiful companion, a furry friend named Mili
She is also amazed by the glamorous view and has almost the same characteristics as me—her owner

Both living a tranquil lifestyle and wanting to live in harmony
We both accommodate the need of another as well as her needing me as well as me needing Mili

She uplifts me as if no one can
She has a humorous character which makes me chuckle and is loyal as one can be.

21
Don't give up on Your Dreams

Dreams almost come true
Wanting to begin dreaming the realisation

Work ethic and motivation is needed to complete your dream
Longing for this dream to happen

Dedication is needed for this desire to happen
One can only try and try

Never give up, which is key
Keep fighting

Anything is possible.

22
Trapped within Walls

Enclosed through a small, enclosed area
Although there is warmth, light and shelter
Still feels like an imprisonment

Counting down the days
When will we leave this misery and the day that it will end?

Those days have passed; even being through it
Triggers many memories

Deceit between the walls and loyalty is even found
Great sadness is encountered being far from anything that we loved before

The walls are a distant memory, as every memory vanishes and leaves
Scarred from those moments

Time will heal the scars which can't be visually seen
Moving forward and scattering and banishing those difficult encounters is key
One should think of the present and future and forget the past
We can't change the past, but we can strive for the present and future.

23
Finding My Soul Mate

My heart desires to meet you, my future soul mate
Through my uplifting and sorrowful moments

Just want to be loved eternally

I hope you think about me ever if we depart away from each other
Even though proximity through affectionate hugs and smiles

Wanting to find my soul mate

Time is not the issue, as individuals will find the right soul mate

24
A journey throughout life

Life becomes tiresome
Days drag
A minute almost feels an hour

Anxiety is stricken
All the unwanted feelings come back and forth

A teardrop comes slowly dropping down the face, feeling upset, guilt and sadness

There are times of happiness, sometimes distressing feeling overriding one's emotions and how one feels

Seeing others full of life makes one happy although lost and does not know where to turn

One wishes of a stable relationship; however, feeling of one's own problems hinders one's emotions

One's image being in a different state of mind where laughter and good times are to happen

One day, happiness will appear, and great memories will be created.

25
Hurt

The feeling of anguish and relief

Realisation and victory through one's pride and dignity

Let me move on

Frustration
Anger
Feelings of betrayal and hurt

Not being listened to

Another being vindictive, their pure hatred and envy due to this individual
Treatment of humiliation made by the other

"You will not humiliate me."

"You will not take it."

Tough!

26
The Lady in Red

A lot of feud, confliction and tension
Ruminating the room

Thrilled for her acquiesce, however had
her foes

Life seemed like a struggle however
She had her ups and downs

Sometimes, there seemed to be no equality or justice playing
her part

Aid was approaching her way
One must learn to be patient

Overwhelming emotions manoeuvring, circulating different
days, months and specific years
Increased palpitations, feeling stricken by anxiety

The lady in red was strong, motivated, and determined to fight for her rights.
Nothing could stop her!

Even through her overwhelming moments
She perceived and carried on!

Whatever life brings you
remember to carry on

Stay strong and great things will happen even if you go through hardship.

27
The Birds

Birds circulating in the air
Early hours of the morning silence
Then suddenly a flock of birds manoeuvring in one set of direction
Their squawking echoing across the sky

The cluster of birds still amongst one another squawking however
Now through a distance as they are further by

My cat fascinated by the birds and jumps on the windowsill and scrutinises their every move

Eventually the birds vanish and there is silence again

It's the season of winter individuals dressed from head to toe
Looking out the window
There are individuals walking, with the cold being -2 degrees
Due to this weather, they walk with haste.

28
1960

Differentiating between individuals whether from culture, ethnicity, race, etc...

The great westerns of all, full of wacky humour, moral to their stories and one of the greatest times and enjoyable movies of that time

A bit of a generational difference, however loved by many, even if not in the generation

Westerns such as the one with the title *'Those Magnificent Men in Their Wackiest Ship in the Army'*
Although not in my generation is a great film of the past.

Made in the USA
Monee, IL
03 May 2026

49438103R00026